I0519463

LIFE
IS A JOKE
AND IT AIN'T EVEN
FUNNY

RIYA AARINI

Life Is a Joke and It Ain't Even Funny

Text copyright © 2024 by Riya Aarini

All rights reserved. No part of this book may be reproduced, distributed or transmitted in any form or by any means, including photocopying, recording, or other electronic or mechanical methods, without prior written permission of the publisher, except in the case of brief quotations embodied in critical articles and reviews. Thank you for the support of the author's rights.

The contents of this book are for entertainment purposes only and not intended to be [good] advice.

Paperback ISBN: 978-1-956496-43-7

eBook ISBN: 978-1-956496-44-4

Library of Congress Control Number: 2024903763

First published in Austin, Texas

www.riyapresents.com

CONTENTS

PART I: OBSERVATIONS ON MATTERS OF SIGNIFICANCE IN THE WORLD

Trying to be likeable is like trying to pay more taxes than you owe.

It's a bit disappointing that zucchini noodle salad has absolutely no noodles in it whatsoever.

There are $20 pillows that give you a good night's sleep. There are $60 pillows that give you an even better night's sleep. Then there are $250 pillows that keep you awake at night wondering why you spent the equivalent of a brief stay at a four-star luxury hotel with a view of the Pacific in every direction, heated floors, lush linens, and a promise of blissful rest and relaxation.

Judge a man by his questions, especially the ones he types into Google.

Life dumps heaps of cow manure onto the front yards of the homes of many unwitting folks. We all handle crap in one of two ways. The foolish complain and cry hopelessly about the stink. But the wise hold their noses, bag it up, and sell it for a premium as fertilizer, retiring early and happily wealthy.

If opportunity doesn't knock, check your phone. It might be texting you.

Friendly bros who gather in the kitchen and pressure fry a marinated chicken until it's juicy and crisp prepare what is known as a broasted chicken.

The young say, "Every day is a chance to be better." The middle-aged say, "Eh, I'm good enough already."

These days, no one gets the show on the road—they take it online.

Some people are a pain in the neck. Others demand a full-body pain reliever.

Having a monkey on your back is more of a worry in South and East Asia than anywhere else.

There is no elevator to success on the forty-fifth floor. You have to take the stairs. Who wants to climb forty-five flights of stairs?

Offer any self-respecting person a penny for their thoughts, and they'll politely decline. But offer a substantial number of dollars, and they'll prepare to negotiate.

Accountants balance the books. The rest of us read them.

There used to be no shortcuts to success. These days, you can consult your GPS for the fastest route.

Heaven must be a fabulous place because no one ever bothers to return to Earth.

A lot of things come before success—even in the dictionary: disappointment, discouragement, failure, and futility. The difference between a dictionary and life, however, is that in a dictionary, with enough scrolling, you are guaranteed to reach success, eventually. In life, there is no such guarantee.

A friend who never pays you back is not a friend but a charitable organization whose fiscal responsibility you should've first assessed with Charity Navigator.

The grass is greener on the other side because it puts up with a lot more rain over there.

Flattery will get you nowhere, except on the narcissist's VIP contacts list.

None of us have a future—it's just an abstract concept. All we can honestly bank on is the present, which is why we try to wrap it up in the prettiest paper and top it off with the biggest, fanciest bow.

Pugs consistently wear a worried expression because they know humans screwed them over with breed manipulations that give them concerningly unhealthy facial characteristics.

Strangely, many of us seek opportunities to bowl over with our hands clutching our stomachs tightly, squeeze our eyes shut as they uncontrollably pool with tears—and enjoy the agony of a good laugh.

It's ironic, when the Man Upstairs gives us troubles, we move closer to him. Yet, when a neighbor gives us troubles, we immediately build an eight-foot-high fence and, at the slightest irritation more, stick a for sale sign in the front yard and move 2,000 miles to the opposite side of the country without regret.

Sexy people are simply defined as those who flaunt a healthy ability to reproduce.

Builders ache, sweat, and toil for months to construct the winding back roads. But crooners with a charming vocal twang sing about the old back roads for just under five minutes, please millions of fans at once, earn a wealth of riches, and give themselves a very comfortable living for life.

The concept of reuniting with loved ones in heaven is murky and complex. What should we expect in cases of unrequited love?

Success does not come before work in any English-language dictionary, but it does so in every Spanish-language dictionary.

At eighty-two, Geoffrey took care of the trailer park in the humble town of Waterloo. He didn't drive a car, but he leisurely rode his lawn mower past the bar so he could people-watch from afar. Geoffrey was a content old man, never wanting more than he had. His pride and joy were his model cars and trains that he spent hours to neatly arrange. But behind his sparkly eyes and mischievous grin was a secret known only to him. When he quietly died a "pauper," he surprised the whole town with a proffer. Without a peep or holler, he left them four million dollars for the benefit of education, health, and culture. To this day, Geoffrey is fondly remembered as the modest millionaire who's riding a mower in heaven somewhere.

You are my sun, my moon, and all my stars—in other words, every time I look at you, it's like gazing through the Hubble Telescope.

Self-improvement programs have a subtle way of bringing out the awful feeling that you're not quite good enough. No one goes into a program saying, "I'm great!" then adds, with a confident smile, "I just want to be even greater."

Reports paint the picture of the number of children per family. When parents have 1.64 children, who exactly makes up the 0.64?

Running around doing everything is tiring. Paradoxically, sitting around doing nothing is more tiring.

If you stand to be comfortably rich, you likewise stand to be uncomfortably rich. At what dollar amount does the uneasiness arise? Uncomfortably rich person: "I'm good with 10 million dollars or even 1 billion dollars, but 2.5 billion dollars is tipping the scale toward discomfort and must be reduced immediately."

It's hard to turn on a dime. It's hard enough to turn on a unicycle.

The Great People Shortage is a boon for unborn children who never have to pay taxes.

If love awakens your soul, hopefully it's more like the gentle awakening from a sunrise alarm than the jarring blaring of the beeping kind that sounds like a truck backing up into your bedroom at 6 a.m.

There's always light; to find it, we must be brave enough to traverse the darkness to the other side of the room and flip on the switch.

What did photogenic people do before the invention of cameras?

Manipulators are either stupid enough to attempt to pull a ruse, or they assume you're stupid enough to fall for one. They rely heavily on sheer stupidity one way or the other.

It always seems impossible until some wise guy shows up and makes it possible.

Life once had no remote—these days we have smartphones that accomplish nearly everything remotely.

If your heart skips a beat every time you think of her, immediately schedule an AI electrocardiogram to check for potential arrhythmias.

Why do some stand-up comedians insist with a streak of defiance to bring an alcoholic drink on stage? It's like they play up the fact that they're the only profession that can't be fired for drinking on the job.

Wealthy people are millionaires. Millionaires are wealthy people. Combining both terms and calling yourself a wealthy millionaire is just shameless bragging.

For the unfortunate, life is hell. For the fortunate, it's a hell of a life.

The way to a man's heart is through his stomach, which is a needlessly roundabout path—and to make matters worse, on your way, you risk getting hopelessly lost somewhere in the liver. But the way to a woman's heart is always straightforward and direct: it's simply through her heart.

It's surprising when a highly intelligent person doesn't know the answer, but it borders on shocking when Google doesn't know the answer.

Having to feed a cold is a dreadful financial hassle for a person living on a fixed income, as it means that, for the duration of the cold, they're stuck with another mouth to feed.

It's simultaneously alarming and comforting when AI diagnoses an ailment with greater speed and accuracy than a medical school graduate with eight years of specialty healthcare experience.

Just when you think you're about to learn about a new case of farm animal cruelty, you discover that the latest "pig butchering" schemes involve no pigs or butchering whatsoever.

Tacos are delicious. But whoever designed the traditional taco shell had no clue about the forces of gravity. The minute you bring the narrow part of the taco up for a bite, half the filling falls out the other end. A taco just isn't a taco without its filling. Then there's the whole difficulty of sitting the tacos up after filling them. Recently, someone came up with the ingenious idea to form flat-bottomed tacos that actually sit upright on the plate like they're supposed to. Still, two open ends don't make for a tidy lunch. Hopefully, this latest invention catches on and proves the immediate and urgent need for taco shell reengineering. Now, whoever invented the snug burrito wrap definitely knows a thing or two.

Choose a partner carefully. A significant other—with the ability to break your heart, send it fluttering, or make it skip a beat—has a powerful influence over your cardiovascular health.

Life, like plays, consists of three acts: birth, convoluted drama, and death.

Trust life's timing, but question it during the frenzy around Daylight Savings Time.

It used to be that a picture was worth a thousand words. These days, a selfie is worth a thousand likes.

Sex sells—in movies, music, and books. Furthering the prospects of human life on Earth earns big bucks.

The world's biggest online retailer, with their own modern fleet of snazzy delivery trucks, is so big that it almost usurps the role of Kriss Kringle. The good news is that they deliver packages and joy every single day *but Christmas*. Good ol' Saint Nick hasn't been toppled yet.

Comedian to a gushing fan: "I'm glad my pain is your joy."

At the end of the day, opinions don't matter. At the beginning of the day, opinions don't matter. Opinions don't rise in value, no matter what part of the day it is.

The inhabited world is the same everywhere. Same good. Same evil. Different accents.

It's a relief that you hear, "I'm a doctor, but I do a little baking on the side"—but you never hear, "I'm a baker, but I practice a little medicine on the side."

"Failure was never an option," said no failure ever.

15

Why do spammers insist on emailing and telling us what they're in the mood for? Most of us don't want to know what a swindler across the world in Vietnam, Poland, or Russia is in the mood for—whether that's pizza, a sandwich, or something as scandalous as rum cake.

Of course, money grows on trees. Ever heard of money trees? They require general-purpose fertilizer and thorough watering and bring you all the wealth in the world: good luck, prosperity, and love.

People who habitually dole out bad advice should never talk to themselves.

Scammers avoid the emails of lonely people like the plague. Their contact list is barren, meaning, for all their efforts, con artists have no opportunity to cheat them out of even one measly gift card.

If you ever feel that you're not good enough, that you're a total mess, that the world stinks, there's an effective remedy guaranteed to cure your blues: browse the wackiest online personal classified ads and instantly feel like one of the most grounded, well-balanced people to ever walk the planet.

Some lucky people have a knack for success. Conversely, some luckless people have a knack for failure.

Oysters are among the most notable of ocean life because they produce pearls of wisdom.

Disguising a bland vegetable as a tasty grain makes it no more palatable. Case in point: cauliflower rice, a faux rice that doesn't cut it, no matter how finely you chop it.

Ugliness is a godsend because it protects your virtue.

One garage door repairman to another in heaven: "I told you I smelled gas."

The delete button must be the most useful invention in modern technology for the preservation of happiness.

Success is when a crowd holds up your book with your face on the cover—*and* they're all smiles.

The millionaire down the street is a man you might happen to meet. He takes his coffee at the local café but deliberately parks one hundred feet away. As such, he avoids feeding the meters, and in winter, he doesn't turn up the heaters. He appears so down on his luck that the lady sitting next to him gives him a buck. He's the keep-to-himself gent who lives with immeasurable content. But when he dies, he leaves his entire wealth behind. A mere sliver goes to his surprised nephew and niece, who find it in themselves to finally make their peace. But his millions in cash boosts his alma mater's stash. You never know when you might run into an honest millionaire—they're one of a kind and exceedingly rare.

If a mirror holds a bit of your soul, stay out of shopping mall dressing rooms—unless you want your soul to be forever remembered in that calico-colored spaghetti strap summer dress you're glad you had enough style sense not to purchase.

If only ancient Egyptians knew to whistle at the sun during a drought to bring much-needed rain. This Norwegian superstition might have saved the Nile from drying up too soon.

Oftentimes, ordinary people are put in extraordinary situations and flat-out fail. At rarer times, extraordinary people are put in extraordinary situations and surprise us all.

If basic bike helmets designed specifically to prevent head injuries are recalled because they specifically pose a risk of head injuries, you apparently can't trust any consumer products these days.

Friend 1: "I don't take myself too seriously."

Friend 2: "How'd you acquire such admirable humility?"

Friend 1: "It's easy. No one else takes me seriously either."

Vegetarian: Consuming fish is harmful and unjust.

Pescatarian: Grizzly bears in the wild devour salmon straight from the river, making civilized people no less justified in enjoying fish.

People who contribute to the slang dictionary corrupt the English language. Innocent words are forever bungled. A chef in the kitchen can't even say, "Give her an onion," without sounding lewd.

Curious Person: "Why are doorknobs so dumb?"

Enlightened Person: "Because they're made of dense material."

Racism is a social evil that follows humanity through the centuries, as resources remain limited and competition is high. When an imminent segment of the population colonizes Mars and alters biologically into a new race due to adapting to living in space, life will be characterized as the Martian race against the race of Earthlings. Rather than the absurd racism we experience today between members of *the same human race*, humanity is destined for a future of racism between two truly distinct races.

Parent feigning concern: "You're having a break with reality."

Least favorite adult child: "That's a relief, because my reality is persistently painful."

On overpopulation: volcanoes, floods, earthquakes, hurricanes, pestilence—Mother Earth is constantly attempting to unload her weighty burden by spontaneously purging large segments of humankind.

Sign of an HMO endodontist: when the surgical needle breaks during a root canal, and, instead of telling you, the endodontist leaves it in the canal—then gives you a guilty-looking fist bump afterward.

It's ironic how people who think they know it all are among the stupidest in the world.

There are no two ways about failing. People who fail fall flat on their backs. It's always better to forward fail, where you fall flat on your face instead.

Listening to the clock ticking is like listening to the sound of Death steadily approaching.

It's a paradox that the more you stay away from doctors and hospitals, the healthier and safer you are.

Many successful and highly sought-after people feel the drudgery in attending speaking engagement after speaking engagement in some fancy hotel seven hundred miles away. They'd rather be at home curled up next to a crackling fire with a good book and a glass of red wine. Failures, on the other hand, circumvent the whole success route and sit at home curled up next to a fire with a good book on any given day, completely free from the drudgery felt by their less-enviable, more successful peers.

It's tough being a kid when stupid adults make stupid decisions for you. It's no better as an adult when stupid politicians make stupid decisions that unhinge your world.

It's bewildering how a smiling baby can instantly transform a tight-lipped, dignified, antsy woman into a babbling, unladylike, easygoing jumble of joy.

South American drug cartels are getting impressively creative, relying on daily fruit exports to transport their pricey goods across the Atlantic Ocean. At one point, they smuggled drugs through entry ports via large shipments of limes. Cleverly disguised balls of cocaine were artistically painted an alluring bright green, even giving off that splendid lime sheen. Most recently, drug cartels advanced, turning to good ol' bananas to smuggle their illegal goods to the United Kingdom and Europe. If sweet Auntie Louise in the UK accidentally got a hold of one of the smuggled limes from the local supermarket and prepared to bake a flavorful key lime pie, she'd say, "What an odd-looking lime!" Then, with a dismissive wave of her hand, she'd shave the rind into her pie. Or perhaps Grandma Magdalene in the Czech Republic unwittingly mashed bananas with a brief history of sitting between bags of cocaine that contaminated the lush yellow fruit. In either case, the lovely ladies would enjoy unprecedented receptions to their baked goods. "Louise, your sensational key lime pie leaves me swooning for more!" and "Magdalene, after eating your marvelous banana bread, I've never felt so euphoric!"

It's always admirable when billionaires ask the public for donations when their bank accounts hold one-fifth of all the money in the world.

Negative people live by one guiding principle: "Never look at the bright side. It's blinding. Ever try looking at the sun?" Surprisingly, they have a point.

The ideal world population is 2 to 3 billion, according to knowledgeable hypothesizers. At the current population of 8 billion, we are fast approaching Earth's maximum carrying capacity of 9 billion people. This means 5 billion people are hanging on as moochers, using up the earth's limited supply of valuable resources, and putting everyone at risk for complete extinction within the next 50 years.

By the time the trusty virus protection indicates that it found your info in 14 breaches, your info is really in 140,000 breaches and dancing to the point of no return in the shadows around the dark web.

Why are carpet beetles called carpet beetles? Is it because their larvae eat carpets, along with other materials, such as feathers, felt, and fur? That's like calling young Italians pasta people, when they also eat risotto and cheese; or young Indians rice people, when they also eat naan and potatoes; or the young Chinese noodle people, when they also eat dumplings and sweet and sour pork. The naming conventions of entomologists are limited in scope and at times misleading.

Heated floors are an ultimate dream. They eliminate the need to make strategic hops from the carpeting to a well-placed series of throw rugs on the way to the bathroom on a cold winter night.

The phrase "the customer is always right" must've been coined by none other than a demanding, irate, and impossible-to-satisfy customer.

Restaurant waiters' level of excellence in service is rated by tips. But customers are never conversely rated, which makes the entire service industry unfairly imbalanced. Nevertheless, waiters have unfortunately devised their own devious ways of rating unreasonable customers and gloating in the satisfyingly sweet taste of revenge not found in the richest sriracha maple bacon sundaes.

If we celebrate failure as lavishly as we celebrate success, it would resolve 85 percent of the self-esteem issues plaguing the developed world.

Global warming has caused the Earth's temperatures to rise noticeably. Yet the men's fashion trend of wearing sophisticated suits hasn't altered in two centuries. Summer temperatures are hotter than they've been in recorded history, but wearing long-sleeved button-up shirts under thick long-sleeved suits still remains accepted by fashion-backward thinkers who have no inclination to devise a form of professional wear "suitable" for the times. As a bold response to the intolerable heat, togas ought to make a comeback. Breezes waft through the loose layers, providing a much-needed cooling effect, all while delivering a sensible sense of style. The ancient Romans were right about so many things.

The other night, a giant extraterrestrial-looking roach, known as the American cockroach, sauntered out of the closet, stretched its wings, yawned as if it were Sunday morning, then proceeded to make its way across the floor like it owned the place.

Have mercy on Grandpa on his eighty-first birthday, and don't light eighty-one flaming candles on his two-layer butterscotch cake. Even with a reduced lung capacity, he'll make the valorous attempt to blow out every single one. And opting for eighty-one trick candles borders on elder abuse.

Some things are about as good as terrible.

The Guinness World Record for the most candles on a cake is 72,585. Due to serious fire safety issues, those candles are unlikely to have topped the Guinness's largest wearable cake dress.

The Caribbean's four-star hotel restaurants are known to provide travelers with an authentic dining experience. That's why they serve fine Italian cuisine, from cheese and antipasti platters to house-made pasta, sizzling American steaks, and dishes inspired by Mediterranean ingredients—everything but Puerto Rican rice and beans, pizza Cubano, and Caribbean jerk chicken—genuine Caribbean food.

Ever wonder how ants react when one of their own has died? "Back, back! Ant down! Ant down!" Later in the break room at the nest: "It was Petey." Ant shaking its antennas, "He got the dreaded shoe."

The downside of taking a 7-day cruise is that you're stuck at sea within the confines of a 1,000-foot ship with 2,000 other passengers who are stuck at sea within the confines of a 1,000-foot ship.

Flashing bedroom eyes is suggestive. But flashing kitchen eyes is definitely an invitation to the table for a steaming pot pie. And flashing yard eyes is an unabashed signal that the lawn needs mowing pronto.

Why can't we serve roaches eviction notices? Is it because they don't pay rent?

In favor of eviction, cockroaches' loud nesting activity is disturbing; they damage the property; and the building itself is intended to be pet-free (most people, except for a few folks who oddly elect to keep them as low-maintenance love bugs, would never consider a roach a pet). Roaches aren't entitled to squatter's rights either: by spreading damage and disease, they don't treat the home like the owner does and therefore can't physically possess the property. However, they do make their presence known so much so that even the owner notices they're living there. Okay, so the roaches can't make a hostile claim, because it's clear they *have* to know that the property belongs to someone else. Why else would they sneak out only under the cover of nightfall? Plus, their occupancy is not exclusive; they share the home with legions of other cringeworthy roaches—this alone invalidates their adverse possession claim. Anyway, since roaches live a maximum of a few months to a year, they lack the lifespan to claim adverse possession; they're simply unable to occupy the home for ten uninterrupted years, even without paying property taxes—which they definitely *don't*.

The biggest promise of AI in the surgical field is accuracy. Unlike a distracted surgeon who suffers from sleep deprivation, emotional stress, or the monotony of performing a continuous seven-hour surgical procedure, there's little chance that AI will remove a left kidney when the right kidney has to go.

Hearing "I feel great, doc!" from patients is a professional death sentence for medical doctors and makes them cringe. Without a regular stream of sick patients stumbling through their doors, they can no longer pay the mortgages on their six-bedroom houses, afford the latest luxury sports cars, or send their kids to pricey prep schools. This explains them ordering excessive tests, performing unnecessary procedures, and prescribing needless drugs—all of which help them detect the slightest symptom that will coerce you back into their impeccably sterile offices. Even if nothing serious is found after a series of invasive pricking and probing, the doctors invent some nonsense, and off you go for another round of tests. Instead of advising a patient with one simple sentence to stop overusing a basic nutritional supplement because it's doing more harm than good, $800 worth of testing, 50 pages of documents from the health insurance company, and a needless fear of an imminent death must precede it. Furthermore, such so-called "care" helps them feel like their four years of medical school plus three years of residency are worth all the trouble—but of course, it's all done at the expense of the perfectly healthy patient.

Physician visits in America are needlessly expensive. Why pay $350 for less than fifteen minutes of a doctor's time, their disastrous attention span, a grumbled response, and their hasty exit out the exam room door? Instead, it's far more cost-effective to consult AI for a diagnosis and possible course of treatment. AI provides an unbiased, straightforward, and reliable solution to cases of cheilitis or diverticulitis or any other "-itis" that happens to temporarily hold your good health hostage.

"Buying a million-dollar fishing lure is the best investment in lazy mornings by the lake," says the fishing lure manufacturer. "Buying 24K gold-plated staples is the best investment in attached documents," says the business owner. "Buying a $1,000 gold leaf sundae is the best investment in dessert," says the restaurateur. "Not buying dross is the best investment you can make in life," says every reasonable person.

Each life is a story. Some are mysteries, many are romantic comedies, and a few are horror stories. The best ones . . . well, you simply can't put them down.

The journey of a thousand miles begins with a trusty GPS, unless you don't mind taking the long, roundabout route and unintentionally ending up right where you started.

Many people think they have something to say. The differentiating factor among them all is whether people want to listen.

A leaf blower is a clearly useful maintenance tool, blowing dead leaves from one spot in the yard to another. The wind simply couldn't do any better.

The journey to earning a million dollars starts with earning one dollar.

Some people are so devoid of compassion that trying to seek it from them is like attempting to extract honey from a brick wall.

The war is on after a long Arizona dry spell followed by a sudden rain. Homeowners arm themselves with specialized tactical gear—an MK-45 flyswatter and a BR-23 can of roach repellent—and execute a sound military strategy to rid their home of the invading two-inch roaches looking to squat on drier ground.

The present is a gift to be opened with a feigned look of pleasant surprise.

Heritage and history months are established to foster inclusion in a remarkably diverse humanity. Yet these few-and-far-between months have the unintended opposite effect by creating tidy divisions. We forget to honor Caribbean Americans in November because their month is in June. We must patiently wait until April to honor the contributions of Arab Americans, May to recognize the efforts of Asian Americans and Pacific Islanders, and March to celebrate the courage of women— or was it August? The scribbled-in calendars of open-minded individuals are a tad confusing. All we need is to set aside one unforgettable month: Human Heritage Month, during which every person on Earth feels wholeheartedly welcome. That way, we can celebrate all of us: the good, the bad, and the terrible.

Can you live the American dream in Mexico, Nova Scotia, or Singapore?

Headless ghosts are the best. They won't talk your head off all night.

The reason that wicked witches are green is that they suffer from an acute case of hypochromic anemia.

When search engines have birthday celebrations as big as those of ten-year-olds, you begin to realize how rapidly AI is taking over the wholesomeness of the human spirit.

Health and happiness are priceless. But they do cost a lot in therapy bills.

Unlike the rest of us, morticians and other professionals who deal with the dead daily have little fear of ghosts. It's actually a job requirement, essential for those dark, lonesome evenings in the funeral home when there's no one between them and the corpse to which they're carefully tending.

Some polite folks are very hesitant to say they don't like other people. The reality is that some people are just not that great.

Today's car thieves can duplicate a key fob's code in seconds from afar. They're as skilled as professional security technicians earning $150,000 annually. These comparatively proficient car criminals work for the lowest pay, plus the risk of prison time. In all likelihood, they simply enjoy the perks of *remote* work.

Stoneman Willie was horribly broke and silly. He lay in peace for 128 years after dying from an equally large number of beers. Lying in an open coffin, he looked almost thirty-somethin'. He was the life of the funeral parlor and, once mummified, caused quite the stir. While he was alive, Willie had no pride; he enjoyed respect only after he died. At last, he's properly laid to rest, and we celebrate him as one of the best. It goes to show that in life you can be a bum—but in death you are someone!

It's not a dog-eat-dog world. Canines are not habitually cannibalistic. To say, "It's a chimp-eat-chimp world," has more basis in factual reality.

How many times does a food stylist have to slice a chocolate-dipped caramel apple to get that single picture-perfect, no-loose-crumbs catalog photo? Most importantly, who gets to eat all the ugly slices?

Celebrities never fail to make the inhuman effort to be positive, regardless of their dire situation. A sweaty performer dressed in a 60-pound head-to-toe costume lifts off her weighty mask to respond to the host's inquiry into how she's feeling. Her reply: "Whew, it was really hot in there!" Then immediately afterward comes the positive spin: "But it was great, you know; I didn't pass out or die of asphyxiation from the 175-degree heat wave inside the costume." A thousand-watt grin promptly follows.

The fact that poorly made products have the potential to be incredibly successful with the help of first-rate advertising fills many below-average creators with splendiferous hope.

Monogamous couples have trouble putting up with even one partner. It's a testament to the extent of human tolerance when polyamorous individuals purposely endure multiple partners.

In a cemetery closely packed with gravestones, for a misanthrope, it's far from "rest in peace"—instead, it's misery for all eternity.

PART II: IF TALK IS CHEAP, A DICTIONARY MUST BE WORTHLESS

S outherners get you excited by saying, "I'll tell you
what," and then flat-out disappoint by stopping short
of telling you anything whatsoever.

Today's youth are getting lazy, which comes off in their
speech. Things that are the "greatest of all time" are
reduced to a bleating farm animal: GOAT. And bothering
to say five words requires too much effort when they
can get by with five letters instead: IYKYK (if you know
you know) and the lazier ones only three: TBH (to be
honest). Some fresh terms have mysterious origins, like
"sleep on," which guiltily out-of-date older generations
associate with things that have to do with a bed, a
pillow, and a cozy blanket. And the Brits who have held

centuries-long traditions of afternoon tea should watch their words these days because to younger folks, "tea" suggests a cup of the latest gossip. Mind you, if you "spill the tea," no one will hand you a paper towel but instead expect you to reveal the up-to-the-minute chatter about who's who and where's where. For heaven's sake, if you're "thirsty," the youth won't serve you a refreshing drink but insist you're trying to get attention. Carpenters can't get on with their jobs because "tools" apparently refer to rude and stupid people. How do you even pronounce "periodt"?

Talk is cheap for spendthrifts but expensive for the pithy who never waste their words.

For postal workers in the US, "neither snow nor rain nor heat nor gloom of night stays these couriers from the swift completion of their appointed rounds." While adverse conditions don't stop fearless postal workers, they don't mind slowing deliveries to a crawl—even in nice weather.

Talk is cheap or ridiculously pricey, depending on what you say, how you say it, to whom you say it, and when. It's the difference between casual and fine dining, where what matters is the food you order, how it's prepared, who's eating it, and at what time of day. Illustratively, it's the difference between a steak sandwich at 2 a.m. in an empty joint and a buttered filet mignon at sunset on the patio of a posh steakhouse.

A "hill of beans" isn't worth much to Southerners but has incredible nutritional value to vegetarians.

"Gimme some sugar" may be a plea for affection in the South. But practical folks in the North take it as, "Bring me that cup of sugar for this pitcher of lemonade I'm mixing."

What do Southerners who think something is as "annoying as all get out" say when they actually want a bunch of annoying people to all get out?

As Southerners know, "you can be a rooster one day and a feather duster the next," or "a tree one day and a wall calendar the next."

Whatever Southerner leisurely said, "It'll all come out in the wash," never had major life problems or even minor issues with the functionality of a washing machine.

People in the South are known especially for their strong religious beliefs. Even when they call you "out-of-your-mind stupid," they say it in the most angelic way: "Why, bless your heart."

New York is a very complex city with language that is no less complicated, considering "yeah, nah" means "no" and "nah, yeah" means "yes." It's literally the confusingly contradictory responses of "yes, no" and "no, yes" to straightforward Midwesterners.

In the South, we say, "I'm fixin' to," but in New York, we say, "I'm finna," and in the Midwest, we make it abundantly clear that "I'm just gonna eat this whole pizza."

Friend 1: "I haven't seen you in a minute!"

Friend 2: "You're exaggerating. It took at least four minutes for the barista to prepare our coffee order."

If a New Yorker believes a "snack" refers to an attractive person, what exactly does he consider pretzels?

New Yorkers consider "cheese" to be money, which explains the fact that The Empire State, with its 4,000 dairy farms, has an impressively high number of millionaires.

Staten Islanders may say someone slightly off their rocker is "gagootz," in other words, gone gaga or simply crazy, just as calling someone "stunad" is an innovative way of saying they're stupid.

What do Staten Islanders do when something's on "fire"? Use an extinguisher?

It's a fine line between the meanings of slang when the seemingly innocent question "you good?" simultaneously suggests to a New Yorker either an angry threat to life or a compassionate concern for the welfare of a fellow human being.

A "cruise" has different connotations altogether for senior citizens who book an adventurous four days on the tropical seas and Californians who are just leaving. One type of cruise costs $800, while the other is free, requiring only a will and a way.

Like New Yorkers, Los Angeles natives love to confuse plainspoken Midwesterners who have no clue that "yeah, no" means "no" and "no, yeah" means "yes." Even the slightest forgetfulness of the intended word order can be disastrous: "Would you like extra gravy with that?" asks the West Coast waiter. Shaking his head side to side, the unwitting Midwestern patron with high cholesterol replies, "Um, no, yeah." He's immediately served a generous restaurant helping that promptly sends him to the ER on a stretcher with sudden cardiac arrest.

For Generation Xers, calling in "sick" often requires an employee to make the extended effort to provide the employer with a written notice from a doctor, while "sick" to today's youth has no place in getting off work because it just means "awesome."

Instead of the long-standing practice of showing appreciation by saying a brief and straightforward "thanks," San Franciscans go out of their way to give gratitude by complimenting appearances and saying, "Good looks." Even a kind gesture on a bad hair day can reward you with this validating response. But then again, the West Coast is known for their emphasis on all things involving fashion. In any case, how do they say, "You're welcome"? By responding, "Oh, it's this new pomade. You've got to try it"?

You can order a "scoop" of mint chocolate-chip ice cream in Chicago, or you can "scoop" someone up from the airport in San Diego without tantalizing your tastebuds in the slightest.

You'd think that belonging to the "three commas club" is a rite of passage for editors. But actually, people in Silicon Valley consider anyone with a net worth of $1 billion to be its finest members.

Silicon Valley bros in the computer programming field are aptly known as "brogrammers."

If combining Spanish and English is "Spanglish," is acceptably complying with English "Accomplish"?

PART III: WISE WORDS MADE WISER

WISE WORDS: "If you judge a fish by its ability to climb a tree, it will live its whole life believing that it is stupid." [1] – *Albert Einstein*

WISER WORDS: If you judge a fish by its ability to climb a tree, you must not have spent too much time around marine life.

WISE WORDS: "A journey of a thousand miles begins with a single step." [2] – *Lao Tzu*

WISER WORDS: The longest journey starts with a single step. So does the shortest one.

WISE WORDS: "Guests, like fish, begin to stink after three days." [3] – *Benjamin Franklin*

WISER WORDS: For introverts, guests and fish begin to stink after three hours.

WISE WORDS: "Life is a balance of holding on and letting go." [4] – *Rumi*

WISER WORDS: Life is a balance of holding on and letting go—that's why trapeze artists get life right.

WISE WORDS: "Life isn't about finding yourself. Life is about creating yourself." [5] – *George Bernard Shaw*

WISER WORDS: If life isn't about finding yourself but creating yourself, what on earth is God's job?

WISE WORDS: "There is only one step from the sublime to the ridiculous." [6] – *Napoleon Bonaparte*

WISER WORDS: There's only one step from the sublime to the ridiculous, and there's only one step from insanity to genius. These are the very reasons it's absolutely critical to maintain the stairs.

WISE WORDS: "The secret of success in life is for a man to be ready for his opportunity when it comes." [7] – *Benjamin Disraeli*

WISER WORDS: The secret of success in life is to be ready for opportunity when it arrives—it's probably already texted you a bazillion times.

WISE WORDS: "One who speaks one language is one person, but one who speaks two languages is two people." [8] – *Turkish Proverb*

WISER WORDS: If one who speaks one language is one person and one who speaks two languages is two people, then one who speaks three languages, at three people, is a crowd. And one who speaks four languages might as well take themselves out for a lively group dinner.

WISE WORDS: "When wealth is lost, nothing is lost; when health is lost, something is lost; when character is lost, all is lost." [9] – *Billy Graham*

WISER WORDS: When the earbuds are lost, nothing is lost; when the smartphone is lost, something is lost; when the contacts list is lost, everything is lost.

WISE WORDS: "When you assume, you make an ass out of u and me." [10] – *Oscar Wilde*

WISER WORDS: When you assume, it doesn't make an ass out of you and me. It only makes an ass out of you.

WISE WORDS: "By failing to prepare, you are preparing to fail." [11] – *Benjamin Franklin*

WISER WORDS: Failing to plan is planning to fail. Technically, that's still considered a plan.

WISE WORDS: "One kind word can warm three winter months." [12] – *Japanese Proverb*

WISER WORDS: One kind word warms three winter months and reduces the heating bill. One harsh word gives you the chills all summer and may be relied upon instead of a central cooling system. Words have the power to decrease your cost-of-living expenses all year long.

WISE WORDS: "The meaning of life is to find your gift. The purpose of life is to give it away." [13] – *Pablo Picasso*

WISER WORDS: The meaning of life is to find your gift buried under the stack on the gift table. The purpose of life is to give it away during the next white elephant gift exchange.

WISE WORDS: "The future belongs to those who believe in the beauty of their dreams." [14] – *Eleanor Roosevelt*

WISER WORDS: The future belongs to those who believe in the beauty of sleeping in.

WISE WORDS: "Coming together is the beginning. Keeping together is progress. Working together is success." [15] – *Henry Ford*

WISER WORDS: Coming together is a party. Staying together is a relationship. Working together is a pain for someone who shows no indications of being a team player.

WISE WORDS: "Do not judge me by my successes. Judge me by how many times I fell down and got back up again." [16] – *Nelson Mandela*

WISER WORDS: Do not judge anyone by their successes. Judge them by how many times they fell and how quickly they performed a fall risk assessment when they got up.

WISE WORDS: "Success is not final; failure is not fatal: it is the courage to continue that counts." [17] – *Winston Churchill*

WISER WORDS: Electrocardiogram results are not final; coronary heart disease is not fatal: it is the courage to savor a delicious high-cholesterol diet that counts.

WISE WORDS: "Love is a great beautifier." [18] – *Louisa May Alcott*

WISER WORDS: Love is indeed a great beautifier. Luckily, the beauty industry hasn't figured out a way to bottle it up and offer it for sale at a ridiculously exorbitant price point. Beautification potions and tools are affordable to anyone with a beating heart.

WISE WORDS: "I believe in one thing—that only a life lived for others is a life worth living." [19] – *Albert Einstein*

WISER WORDS: I believe in one thing—that only a life lived for deep-dish chocolate skillet cookies is a life worth living.

WISE WORDS: "Forget the mistake. Remember the lesson." [20] – *Roald Dahl*

WISER WORDS: It's good to forget the mistake and remember the lesson, but it's even better to bypass the mistake altogether and embrace the lesson without going through all the trouble.

WISE WORDS: "The mind once enlightened cannot again become dark." [21] – *Thomas Paine*

WISER WORDS: A mind that has become enlightened cannot become dark, except in unfortunate instances when the whole electrical grid fails.

WISE WORDS: "It's not enough to know how to ride; you must also learn how to fall." [22] – *Mexican Proverb*

WISER WORDS: It's not enough to learn how to ride; you must also learn how to fall—especially when you're on a riding mower and any chance of falling is a grave threat to life and limb.

WISE WORDS: "You've got to find what you love." [23]
– *Steve Jobs*

WISER WORDS: You have to keep looking to find what you love, and sometimes all it takes is an updated optometrist's prescription.

WISE WORDS: "Look deep into nature, and then you will understand everything better." [24] – *Albert Einstein*

WISER WORDS: Look deep into the screen of your pocket translator, and then you will understand everything better.

WISE WORDS: "No man is an island, entire of itself." [25] – *John Donne*

WISER WORDS: No person is an island. That's a relief, as some of us wouldn't want to escape to one if it were.

WISE WORDS: "Man proposes, but God disposes." [26]
– *Thomas A. Kempis*

WISER WORDS: God is the dependable trash collector who empties the bins every Tuesday morning, dutifully crushing dreams in the back of the refuse truck and dumping them in the mountainous landfills overflowing with the rest of the world's hopeful propositions.

WISE WORDS: "It is during our darkest moments that we must focus to see the light." [27] – *Aristotle*

WISER WORDS: It is in our darkest moments that we must focus on finding the elusive light pull on the table lamp that some bozo placed all the way at the opposite side of the room.

WISE WORDS: "Whose house is of glass must not throw stones at another." [28] – *George Herbert*

WISER WORDS: People who live in glass houses should not throw stones, but they should equip themselves with an ample supply of window cleaner.

WISE WORDS: "Those who wish to sing always find a song." [29] – *Swedish Proverb*

WISER WORDS: Just like those who want to sing always find a song, those who want to stir up trouble always find a complaint.

WISE WORDS: "Even though you know a thousand things, ask the man who knows one." [30] – *Turkish Proverb*

WISER WORDS: Even though AI knows a thousand things, ask the human who knows one.

WISE WORDS: "The most important thing is to not stop questioning." [31] – *Albert Einstein*

WISER WORDS: The important thing is to not stop questioning, unless you're pulled over by a police officer for speeding in the fast lane on the highway in the middle of the night, after you left the bar.

WISE WORDS: "The pen is mightier than the sword." [32] – *Edward Bulwer-Lytton*

WISER WORDS: The pen used to be mightier than the sword. These days, the keyboard is mightier than both the archaic sword and the obsolete pen.

WISE WORDS: "For a man's house is his castle." [33] – *Sir Edward Coke*

WISER WORDS: A person's home is their castle. A person's toilet is their throne. We're all royalty here.

WISE WORDS: "The moon is made of green cheese." [34] – *John Heywood*

WISER WORDS: If the moon is made of well-keeping green cheese, that explains how astronaut Neil Armstrong's footprint endures.

WISE WORDS: "He that dies pays all debts." [35] – *William Shakespeare, The Tempest, Act 3, Scene 2*

WISER WORDS: If a debt collector can be satisfied with death, anyone who enjoys life must never go into debt— which takes the life out of living.

WISE WORDS: "Early to bed and early to rise makes a man healthy, wealthy, and wise." [36] – *Benjamin Franklin*

WISER WORDS: Early to bed and early to rise makes a person healthy, wealthy, and wise—says the chipper morning person. Late to bed and late to rise makes a person equally healthy, wealthy, and no less wise—says the night owl, who, by the way, is known especially for its wisdom.

WISE WORDS: "He that wants money, means, and content is without three good friends." [37] – *William Shakespeare, As You Like It, Act 3, Scene 2*

WISER WORDS: He that wants money, means, and content is without three good friends. What classifies as friendship hasn't changed in over five hundred years.

WISE WORDS: "Oh, East is East and West is West, and never the twain shall meet." [38] – *Rudyard Kipling*

WISER WORDS: East is east, and west is west. Who'd have ever thought differently? No one in their right mind says, "Green is green," and actually means, "Green is purple."

WISE WORDS: "A happy man is too satisfied with the present to dwell too much on the future." [39] – *Albert Einstein*

WISER WORDS: A happy man is too satisfied with the smokey barbeque ribs presently on his plate to dwell too much on how it affects his future cholesterol levels.

WISE WORDS: "Hunger is felt by slave and hunger is felt by a king." [40] – *Ashanti Proverb*

WISER WORDS: A king gets hungry. A pauper gets hungry. The difference between the king and the pauper is that, with a ring of his bell, the king is satisfied with a five-course meal promptly cooked and delivered to his table, while the pauper's bell only lends a bit of music to his rumbling tummy.

WISE WORDS: "Eat, drink, and be merry, for tomorrow we die." [41] – *Epicurus*

WISER WORDS: Eat, drink, and be merry, for tomorrow we die. There's nothing better than to die happy and a with a full stomach. A little red wine to offer a final toast to life never hurt either.

WISE WORDS: "For the want of a nail the shoe was lost, / For the want of a shoe the horse was lost, / For the want of a horse the rider was lost, / For the want of a rider the battle was lost, / For the want of a battle the kingdom was lost, and all for the want of a horseshoe nail." [42] – *Benjamin Franklin*

WISER WORDS: For the want of an apple seed, the apple tree was lost, / For the want of the apple tree, the apple was lost, / For the want of the apple, the baker was lost, / For the want of the baker, none of us get a bite of apple pie.

WISE WORDS: "Life is like riding a bicycle. To keep your balance, you must keep moving." [43] – *Albert Einstein*

WISER WORDS: Life is like playing the piano. To hear the music, you have to keep pounding the ivory keys.

WISE WORDS: "Good talk saves the food." [44] – *English Proverb*

WISER WORDS: Good talk saves the food, which is why mediocre dining establishments encourage chatter with tight spaces, Where's Waldo-like paintings, and the strategically timed servings of average meals.

WISE WORDS: "He who can, does. He who cannot, teaches." [45] – *George Bernard Shaw*

WISER WORDS: She who can, does. She who cannot, teaches—which is unfortunately why we have a teacher shortage.

WISE WORDS: "He who laughs last, laughs longest." [46] – *John Heywood*

WISER WORDS: He who laughs last, laughs longest, because he finally gets the joke.

WISE WORDS: "He who lives by the sword, dies by the sword." [47] – *Biblical Proverb*

WISER WORDS: He who lives by the keyboard, dies from sitting too long in front of the keyboard. Yep, sitting too long can kill you.

WISE WORDS: "Hindsight is always 20/20." [48] – *Popular Aphorism*

WISER WORDS: In the US, hindsight is always 20/20. But in Europe, hindsight is always 6/6.

WISE WORDS: "If you can't live longer, live deeper." [49] – *Italian Proverb*

WISER WORDS: If you can't live longer, cryogenics may offer hope.

WISE WORDS: "If you pay peanuts, you get monkeys."

[50] – *James Goldsmith*

WISER WORDS: It's a mistake to think that if you pay peanuts, you get monkeys. Monkeys prefer bananas.

WISE WORDS: "Where ignorance is bliss, 'tis folly to be wise." [51] – *Thomas Gray*

WISER WORDS: Ignorance is bliss. In the Age of Information, none of us with internet access has bliss.

WISE WORDS: "Into each life some rain must fall." [52] – *Henry Wadsworth Longfellow*

WISER WORDS: Into every life a little rain must fall. Ah, how sweet is a drizzle. Unfortunately, torrential monsoons end up flooding some lives to the point of requiring swift and immediate evacuation.

WISE WORDS: "But for mine own part, it was Greek to me." [53] – *William Shakespeare, Julius Caesar, Act 1, Scene 2*

WISER WORDS: While it's Greek to some, it's binary to tech folks.

WISE WORDS: "It is better to light a candle than curse the darkness." [54] – *Eleanor Roosevelt*

WISER WORDS: It is better to turn on a smartphone's flashlight mode than curse the darkness.

WISE WORDS: "Still you keep on the windy side of the law." [55] – *William Shakespeare, Twelfth Night, Act 3, Scene 4*

WISER WORDS: The Windy City's (Chicago's) politicians also keep to the windy side of the law. They're so full of hot air that they put volcano steam to shame.

WISE WORDS: "It takes a thief to catch a thief." – *Popular Saying*

WISER WORDS: It takes a hacker to catch a hacker.

WISE WORDS: "I had rather have a fool to make me merry than experience to make me sad." [56] – *William Shakespeare, As You Like It, Act 4, Scene 1*

WISER WORDS: Fools highly experienced in foolery send you over the moon crying.

WISE WORDS: "Keep cool: it will be all one a hundred years hence." [57] – *Ralph Waldo Emerson*

WISER WORDS: Due to the rapid proliferation of AI in every sector, it will not be the same a hundred years hence—or fifty or twenty. As a matter of fact, even next year will not be the same.

WISE WORDS: "Least said, soonest mended." [58] – *Charles Dickens*

WISER WORDS: Talk therapists and daytime talk show hosts never recommend, "least said, soonest mended," because they don't want to go out of business.

WISE WORDS: "Life really does begin at forty." [59] – *Carl Jung*

WISER WORDS: Life begins at forty, which is discouraging because physical and cognitive decline begin shortly thereafter.

WISE WORDS: "The little foolery that wise men have makes a great show." [60] – *William Shakespeare, As You Like It, Act 1, Scene 2*

WISER WORDS: The little foolery that fools have makes a great internet meme.

WISE WORDS: "Life isn't all beer and skittles." [61] – *Thomas Hughes*

WISER WORDS: Life is not all beer and skittles. For those with a little extra spending money, it's chardonnay and chocolate truffles.

WISE WORDS: "Life is what you make it." [62] – *Eleanor Roosevelt*

WISER WORDS: Life, just like a ham sandwich, is what you make it.

WISE WORDS: "Man's evil manners live in brass; their virtues we write in water." [63] – *William Shakespeare, Henry VIII, Act 4, Scene 2*

WISER WORDS: Man's evil ways live on the 24-hour news; their virtues we support with crowd funding.

WISE WORDS: "Avoid your children: small pitchers have wide ears." [64] – *John Heywood*

WISER WORDS: Little pitchers have big ears and even bigger mouths.

WISE WORDS: "Manners maketh man." [65] – *William Horman*

WISER WORDS: If manners make the man, then that's the unfortunate reason slick conmen profit from a smile and handshake.

WISE WORDS: "Money talks." [66] – *Euripides*

WISER WORDS: "Money talks" is not a far stretch of the imagination, since a lot of today's devices get quite chatty too.

WISE WORDS: "If opportunity doesn't knock, build a door." [67] – *Milton Berle*

WISER WORDS: Opportunity doesn't knock until you build a door. But if you have only basic construction skills, patiently wait for opportunity to fly in through the window.

WISE WORDS: "No sooner met but they looked; no sooner looked but they loved; no sooner loved but they sighed; no sooner sighed but they asked one another the reason; no sooner knew the reason but they sought the remedy." [68] – *William Shakespeare, As You Like It, Act 5, Scene 2*

WISER WORDS: Those who've just met, briefly dated, quickly married, leisurely regretted, and underwent respectful mediation sought the remedy via the fastest and least expensive route: uncontested divorce.

WISE WORDS: "Only fools and horses work." [69] – *Cockney Saying*

WISER WORDS: If only fools and horses work, how do the rest of the one percent earn a living?

WISE WORDS: "Let's sit crooked and talk straight." [70]
– *Armenian Saying*

WISER WORDS: Why sit crooked and talk straight when you could sit straight and talk straight just the same without fidgeting uncomfortably to find a way to sit unnaturally crooked?

WISE WORDS: "The fool doth think he is wise, but the wise man knows himself to be a fool." [71] – *William Shakespeare, As You Like It, Act 5, Scene 1*

WISER WORDS: If a wise person knows they're a fool and a fool knows they're wise, then by definition, the wise person clearly acknowledges their complete and utter wisdom.

WISE WORDS: "Him that makes shoes goes barefoot himself." [72] – *Robert Burton*

WISER WORDS: The shoemaker's son always goes barefoot, and the chef's son always goes hungry. These are the reasons both professions experience high rates of job turnover.

WISE WORDS: "They say the best men are molded out of faults, and, for the most, become much more the better for being a little bad." [73] – *William Shakespeare, Measure for Measure, Act 5, Scene 1*

WISER WORDS: Some of the folks who have a history of making repeated mistakes are among the most preeminent of all humankind and should run for office— and many do.

WISE WORDS: "Tell me and I will forget, show me and I may remember; involve me and I understand." [74] – *Confucius*

WISER WORDS: Tell me how to earn a million dollars, and I will forget; show me how to earn a million dollars, and I may remember; involve me in earning a million dollars, and we're both happy millionaires.

WISE WORDS: "When life gives you lemons, make lemonade." [75] – *Elbert Hubbard*

WISER WORDS: When life gives you lemons, promptly return them.

PART IV: ATTRACTING ONLY THE BEST FOR THE JOB

It doesn't bode well for a company when it seeks a bakery manager who enjoys preparing and baking cookies, cakes, and croissants, yet strives to "help people make healthy choices."

Always keep to the contract when working in a contract position, especially when the appointment is not authorized to work an hour more than 999 per year. Failing to comply and working extra in the allotted year can lead to termination. Essentially, all it takes for an employee to be fired is to work.

It's a relief when a delivery driver position stipulates, "no major accidents required," as most applicants don't want to have to get into one to be eligible for the job.

Some healthcare jobs are obstacle courses with frequent bending, reaching, lifting, turning, pushing, and pulling up to forty-five pounds, plus the risk of exposure to radiation and numerous health hazards. Only the fittest and most adventurous thrill seekers need apply.

It's always a sign of a warm and supportive work environment when, right off the bat, one of the job skills required of the applicant is that they "must be able to receive criticism."

Armed security guards may be required at an outdoor post. An outdoor position demands that they possess the physical endurance to withstand heat, humidity, cold and/or snow, sleet, rain, hail, and wind. In other words, the most qualified applicants have the credentials of a marble statue.

A delivery driver job that requires thirty-plus years of continuous driving is unlikely to receive a single application from an individual—as human beings are incapable of driving nonstop safely for even thirty hours. Plus, with an eligibility criterion of thirty-plus years of continuous driving, it automatically rules out anyone under the age of forty-six who'd naturally be fit enough to pass the requisite physical exam.

You know how reliant we've become on phones when a job for a pet boarding facility assistant manager specifically mandates that potential candidates have the capability to work without their cellphone.

The local family friendly pet ranch reveals its priorities when being a dog lover is at a worrisome line twelve of a seventeen-line list of qualifications.

It's necessary for personal trainers to handle any situation without drama, which instantly disqualifies actors from applying for the job.

Retail associates are obligated to welcome and engage with customers in a warm, friendly manner. Anyone who's been inside one of the retail tech giants knows this professional duty only applies when the customer walks in. Otherwise, the retail associates are free to dodge browsing customers and engage solely with customers who are ready to buy and contribute significantly to their sales commission check.

Employees with two left feet always appreciate it when their company's main job perks include unlimited dance parties.

Cashiers / smoke and vape tenders must have several qualifications, including self-motivation, the ability to operate a cash register, as well as the complete and utter disregard for contributing to irreversible lung damage in their vaping customers. Interestingly, the more people they sell vaping products to—thereby increasing the rate of potentially fatal lung cancers—the higher their performance bonus.

One of the biggest benefits of a part-time position is the company provided uniform. Wearing it faithfully seals your deal with them for each nine-hour shift with an hour-long unpaid meal break nestled in for good legal measure.

A company's most attractive job benefit—the onsite medical clinic—is especially useful when an executive chef with an annual salary of $70,000 is forced to work evenings, weekends, and holidays, leading to severe burnout, anger management issues, and stress levels that routinely spike.

Working for an amusement park requires having the ability to work in an environment as fast-paced as their roller coasters, which means filling the condiment dispensers unfazed as dozens of rickety rides speed past at 150 mph in every direction all at once.

It's always critical that baristas serve their customers with a sense of urgency, just like emergency room personnel. We all know how dangerously jittery we get without a promptly served cup of jo in the morning.

Barista job requirements are normally straightforward: food handler certification, weekend availability, and fluency in English. But it catches applicants off guard when they sneak in that one unquantifiable job requirement: "magic." It only makes sense once they realize the company seeks to add fairy godmothers, wizards, good witches, and other fantastical humans to their "magical team."

It's usually a sign of a potentially toxic work environment when the business leaves the Company Values section of their job listing blank.

Working at a major retailer's warehouse can be a dangerous job. That's why it's mandatory that the teams share safety tips daily. Daily? It makes you think new threats, including moving robotic machines with minds of their own, emerge continuously and require spontaneous safety planning by defensive human warehouse workers every single day.

These days, work terminology is a lot less stuffy. Instead of attending formal management meetings, assistant managers now attend casual management huddles.

Notable world leaders, Nobel Peace Prize winners, and global humanitarians are always ready to make a legendary impact. To our pleasant surprise, per the job criteria, hairstylists at the local big box salon franchise must also be prepared to make a legendary impact on the least likely of town residents.

Some jobs are relatively uncommon—like a Cheese Specialist with knowledge of the percentage of total solids and butterfat who works twelve-hour shifts plus overtime in the Cheese Department—but important to the production of our nation's supply of cheeses with zero defects.

It's difficult to attract candidates to a sanitor position working the third shift, which is why companies attempt to lure candidates by asking if they'd prefer to work in an environment with a wonderful aroma. What more could applicants ask for?

You know a Millennial wrote up the job listing when the acronyms "GOAT" and "BOMB AF" are sprinkled throughout the description.

It's always helpful when the job posting for a cook clarifies that it's not a remote position. How great would it be to prepare flawless sunny-side up eggs from a home kitchen dressed in pajama bottoms?

When applying for a part-time job as a barista, it's important to evaluate the working conditions, especially when the employee can expect to work in close proximity to coworkers. The hazards include cuts, minor burns, slips and falls, and tripping. A colleague can send you scrambling, at best, for the first aid kit, and, at worst, to the emergency room.

It's a basic qualification in life, as it is in working in a chicken plant: you "must have the ability to apply common sense."

PART V: COMMONSENSITIZED IDIOMS

If revenge is sweet and revenge is a dish that is best served cold, then revenge must be ice cream.

Cutting a long story short is an editor's pride and passion.

Life is 10 percent crap and 90 percent how quickly you clean it up.

If it really rains cats and dogs, then we have a bigger spay and neuter problem than we realized.

For coffee aficionados, a cup of tea is never their cup of tea.

If you love someone not for who they are but who you are when you're with them, it could be a sign of an identity crisis pending.

Opportunity never knocks twice on any person's door. But it may send multiple texts.

Never ask a man's wage, because it's probably higher than a woman's wage in the still ridiculously inequitable twenty-first century.

If no news is good news, then the good news must be even better.

No one can set the record straight. We can only make it turn.

Some things are right as rain, as no one ever proved raindrops to be wrong.

Why would anyone want to kill two birds with one stone? It's committing animal cruelty twice.

Everyone is under the weather. None of us are above it, literally or morally.

You can be snowed under in Chicago or New York but never in Arizona or Nevada.

When she said he stole her thunder, she exaggerated her sense of ownership. Thunder is a universal weather condition that belongs to no one in particular.

Every day that passes, we call it a day.

Sticking to your guns can be a misfortune, especially in Wild West showdowns, where the cowboy who finds his guns adhered to his hands as soon as he digs into his holster is shot dead first.

Unless it's a clear day, clouds are always on the horizon. It's a natural part of the weather conditions on Earth.

Anyone who is blue in the face is probably dead, or at least close.

When we speak of the devil, we speak of the Almighty right away to balance things out.

Whoever let the cat out of the bag is a compassionate soul, especially compared to the merciless person who stuffed the cat in the bag in the first place.

Some rare things cost an arm and leg, others an abdomen and a neck.

No elephant is ever in the room, because residential doorways aren't built for giant-sized wildlife.

Pretty pennies routinely make their way into the beauty salon cash register.

What most people truly appreciate in a nutshell is the nut, not what's being said.

We're all on top of the world. None of us are under it—except the ones buried six feet deep.

Time is money. So, having a lot of time on your hands and in your pockets makes you filthy rich.

When situations get out of hand, it's time to bring in the foot.

Being two peas in a pod is rather claustrophobic.

The only thing that knows which way the wind blows is the trusty weather vane.

You can catch more flies with honey than with vinegar, but all you're left with is a stickier mess and a bunch of flies you don't know what to do with.

Letting someone off the hook is a horrendous way to treat humanity. Only towels and winter outerwear should be let off the hook.

What exactly is rocket science to a rocket scientist?

It's impossible to give anyone a cold shoulder, unless it's a leftover, refrigerated beef cut primal chuck served on a platter with a sprig of bright green parsley.

If your head is in the clouds, a fog must have descended.

When you pull the last straw, it's not likely to make a difference to a haystack that has been gradually reduced to two or three unremarkable straws of hay anyway.

That ship has sailed, like all ships sailing on the world's oceans do every tourist season.

It's always darkest before dawn, unless you're in Alaska, where daylight shines twenty-four hours on summer days.

You can make an omelet without breaking a few eggs if you opt for liquid eggs from a carton.

When it rains, it pours—except when it's a drizzle.

You can miss the boat, but trust that it will eventually turn around for the return voyage.

Pulling someone's leg should be considered assault.

It's always helpful when you see eye to eye, but even more so when you're looking into the eye of a needle to thread it.

No one should ever wear their heart on their sleeve, as it could take several washings to clean up the shirt.

You can compare apples to oranges. They're both roundish, juicy winter fruits that are tasty in salads.

Pigs never fly, which means nothing impossible ever happens.

Curiosity can be ruthless, especially when it kills innocent animals, such as cats.

You can wrap something, like a scarf, around your head, but you can't wrap your head around anything.

The dry fallen leaves are mostly what get the wind.

No one ever hears anything directly from a horse's mouth, because horses don't speak English or Finnish or Spanish or Lithuanian or any other language that is comprehensible to the human ear.

Who knew that fiddles could be fit? They must enviably get in ten reps of strumming daily.

Many of today's devices are the best things since sliced bread, while even earlier gadgets are the best things before sliced bread.

If you walk a mile in someone else's worn shoes, expect agonizing foot pain a day later.

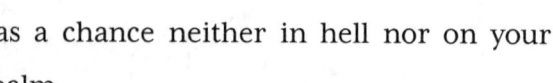

If the devil is in the details, then the Almighty is in the big picture.

A snowball has a chance neither in hell nor on your outstretched palm.

Every cloud has a silver lining or an ominous, dark one.

Biting off more than you can chew can lead to a severe case of indigestion.

Yes, you can have your cake and eat it too. That's the whole intention behind baking a cake. Enjoy.

If you keep your eyes on the stars, you'll slip on a banana peel on the ground.

It's not what life throws at you but how you handle what life throws at you that matters. Some of us don't know how to deal with problems that arrive in the form of an MK48 torpedo raging at us at 230 mph with the ability to differentiate a decoy from the real target.

If the stars hold our destiny, it sure is a long way up to reach it.

Never let an infection get to your head. Never let cholesterol get to your heart.

Being impervious to discouragement means inhumanly going from failure to failure without a loss of enthusiasm.

Success does not come before hard work in any English-language dictionary.

All our dreams can come true if we have the courage to sleep in just a little longer.

If failure is not the opposite of success, then what is?

Success is not the key to happiness, because it fails to unlock even a basic front door.

Success is a journey, not a destination. That's a relief since plenty of us on the journey never get there.

The ladder of success is never crowded at the top—or the middle. If it were, it'd be some ladder.

Good thing love doesn't make the world go 'round. Some of us are prone to sickness with all the spinning.

Where there is love, there is life. Where there is cheese, there are mice. Everything has consequences.

Loving without limits is like speeding without fear of getting a ticket. Both are for the daring.

Don't forget to be awesome, unless you're living with cognitive decline and remembering even today's date is asking considerably much.

Some things unfold in their own time, and the same is true for the clothes we wear.

What's coming is better than what's gone—except when it's a Category 5 hurricane coming at your beachfront home with 157-mile-per-hour winds.

If failure is a part of success, the former takes a whole lot of satisfaction out of the latter.

Love is when you give a person the last piece of steak without them knowing you swiped it off the edge of their plate.

Do not judge by appearances, except when you're looking at the cover of a book and considering whether to spend a hard-earned $9.99.

Curiosity has its own reason for existing, namely, death. Look what happened to the cat who got curious—and it had nine lives to squander.

A person who has never made a mistake has never tried cooking pralines.

Appearances can be deceptive, considering all smartphone cameras come with image enhancers.

Long ago, good things came to those who waited. But given today's technological advances, we experience instant gratifications, making it so that nothing good comes anymore.

Knowledge is power. That's why anyone with Google has power.

If there's no place like home, then not even home is like home.

There is no time like the present and no gift like time.

Why is it that time is money but money is not time? No one buys a loaf of bread with twenty minutes.

Two heads are better than one, which explains why the world is a mess—most of us have only one head.

When in Rome, do as the Romans do. What do Romans do in the rest of the world?

Don't cross the bridge until you come to it. There's really no other way to cross it.

A rolling stone gathers no moss, but it certainly creates a legacy in music.

An apple a day keeps the doctor away, making the juicy red fruit the most affordable health insurance plan for preventive care.

Bad news travels fast, so does good news in the era of email, text, and chat.

"Behind every great man is a great woman," is a highly sexist remark. "Next to every great man stands an equally great woman," is, however, acceptable.

Whomever thinks it's better to reign in hell than to serve in heaven doesn't know how great heaven is.

Can you have Spanish yogurt and Greek tacos? In our cross-cultural world, why has no one thought of these things?

Dead men tell no tales, unless they're Marley from *A Christmas Carol*. Then they fill up three-quarters of the book with them.

Many things are easier said than well-done. And we're not talking about steak.

South, west, home is best—it all makes sense when home is southwest.

Every Jack has his Jill, and what'd you know, they both have their own hill to mow.

Every picture tells a story. These days, it's captioned under or to the right of a social media photo.

Fake it till you make it, unless it comes with a $10,000 plastic surgeon fee.

Fight fire with fire. Or, on second thought, you could just use a fire extinguisher.

Do great minds think alike? Albert Einstein, one of the greatest minds ever to grace humanity, never stooped to think like anyone else. On the other hand, plenty of US politicians think remarkably alike.

If history repeated itself, it wouldn't be history again. It'd be the present.

Since laughter is the best medicine, the heart disease patient in need of quality care is advised to skip the cardiologist's office and plan for a riveting evening at the comedy club.

For some unlucky people, no matter what they do or don't do, they're going to hell in a cheaply made wicker handbasket that's destined to split from the bottom mid-course.

Whoever said less is more never devoured a small paper bag of crisp, freshly fried French fries.

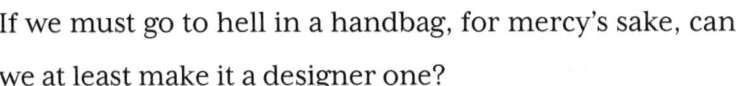

Keep your chin up, especially while shaving, swimming, or engaging in any other activity that's a risk to life or chin.

If we must go to hell in a handbag, for mercy's sake, can we at least make it a designer one?

Laughter is the best medicine. Unless prescribed otherwise, the ill should always remain in laughter compliance to improve their condition. Hospitals and their sick patients stand to benefit from having professional comedians working regular shifts at a higher pay than medical professionals.

Never speak ill of the dead, especially the egotistical ones, because they may rise up to haunt you until you twist the criticism to lavish praise.

Loose lips and, these days, social media posts sink ships and disrupt presidential elections, respectively.

If money makes the world go 'round, the wealthy eccentrics ensure Earth spins.

You are what you eat, which is why it's best to avoid chicken, spotted dick, and beaver tails.

Long ago, marriages were made in heaven. Nowadays, they are made and unmade in courtrooms.

Pride goes before a fall and so does a handsome gentleman (when falling in love) and that cord across the floor (when falling on your face). Pride, cords, and attractive people are all fall hazards we should be regularly cautious about.

Women spend a lot of time fussing over their appearance, including their dress, makeup, and hair. Men are no different, considering a busy crew of nine tailors makes a man.

The saying, "out of sight, out of mind," is true, unless you have ear pods in your ears and everything's within hearing and whirring in your mind.

Practice makes perfect; refrain makes imperfection. Avoiding any ill chance of imperfection is a legitimate reason to not refrain from consuming an entire pizza pie.

Put your best foot forward. And if you're lucky enough to have two great feet, you have a logical reason to leap.

Never put your money where your mouth is. You never know where those dollar bills circulated.

We can all have our cake and eat it too, at birthdays, weddings, anniversaries, and other life milestones. Refusing cake is just inhuman and at worst impolite.

If you see a pin and pick it up, you're pretty lucky that it didn't go through your foot. But if you see a pin and let it lay, you're bound to step on it one unlucky day.

Whoever said there's no such thing as a free lunch has never had the good fortune to be a member of rewards clubs that give out free donuts, ice cream, subs, steak, smoothies, and pizza on birthdays. Then they get not only a free lunch but a free breakfast, midday snacks, and a satisfying four-course dinner.

If the third time is always a charm, is it possible to skip the first and second time and get right to the third?

No one puts the cart before the horse anymore due to simple logistics. These days, the trailer won't even hook up anywhere but behind the truck.

Variety is the spice of life, but it's one spice that's hardest to find in the grocer's baking aisle.

Walls have ears and hidden cameras have eyes.

There are never two sides to every question but two sides to every answer: yours and mine.

There's no fool like an old fool or a young fool or a fool who just turns twenty-one and tries something no thirty-year-old has the guts to try anymore.

"You can have too much of a good thing," said no person with a good thing ever.

Laughter is the best medicine, which is the reason we ought to build comedy care clinics instead of healthcare clinics, fill physician prescriptions for a half-hour of stand-up twice daily until symptoms improve, and get an annual humor checkup to ensure the funny bone is still in good condition.

**

Although *Life Is a Joke and It Ain't Even Funny* might not sell a million copies worldwide and although there's a slight chance it might not snag a nomination for the Nobel Prize in Literature, thank you for reading.

If you could take 5.24 seconds out of your amazing life to leave a review, it'd be much appreciated.
And if that's still asking too much, the author graciously understands.

www.riyapresents.com

BIBLIOGRAPHY

[1] "A Quote by Albert Einstein," n.d., https://www. goodreads.com/quotes/8136665-everybody-is-a-genius-but-if-you-judge-a-fish.

[2] "A Quote by Lao Tzu," n.d., https://www.goodreads. com/quotes/21535-the-journey-of-a-thousand-miles-begins-with-a-single.

[3] "A Quote by Benjamin Franklin," n.d., https://www. goodreads.com/quotes/1297799-guests-like-fish-begin-to-smell-after-three-days.

[4] "A Quote by Rumi (Jalal ad-Din Muhammad ar-Rumi)," n.d., https://www.goodreads.com/quotes/9258541-life-is-a-balance-of-holding-on-and-letting-go.

[5] "A Quote by George Bernard Shaw," n.d., https://www.goodreads.com/quotes/8727-life-isn-t-about-finding-yourself-life-is-about-creating-yourself.

[6] "Napoleon Bonaparte: 'There Is Only One Step From the Sublime to the Ridiculous.' — the Socratic Method," The Socratic Method, November 1, 2023, https://www.socratic-method.com/quote-meanings/napoleon-bonaparte-there-is-only-one-step-from-the-sublime-to-the-ridiculous.

[7] "Benjamin Disraeli Quotes (Author of Sybil, or the Two Nations)," n.d., https://www.goodreads.com/author/quotes/47030.Benjamin_Disraeli.

[8] "Lewis University | Foreign Language | Language Proverbs and Sayings," n.d., https://www.lewisu.edu/academics/foreignlang/proverbs.htm.

[9] "A Quote by Billy Graham," n.d., https://www.goodreads.com/quotes/653548-when-wealth-is-lost-nothing-is-lost-when-health-is.

[10] Jeff Scheinrock, "The Agile Startup: Quick and Dirty Lessons Every Entrepreneur Should Know," O'Reilly Online Learning, n.d., https://www.oreilly.com/library/view/the-agile-startup/9781118744482/xhtml/Chapter02_2.html.

[11] "A Quote by Benjamin Franklin," n.d., https://www.goodreads.com/quotes/15061-by-failing-to-prepare-you-are-preparing-to-fail.

[12] "A Japanese Proverb," Japan Reference, January 25, 2003, https://jref.com/threads/a-japanese-proverb.1519/.

[13] "A Quote by Pablo Picasso," n.d., https://www.goodreads.com/quotes/607827-the-meaning-of-life-is-to-find-your-gift-the.

[14] "A Quote by Eleanor Roosevelt," n.d., https://www.goodreads.com/quotes/6358-the-future-belongs-to-those-who-believe-in-the-beauty.

[15] "A Quote by Henry Ford," n.d., https://www.goodreads.com/quotes/118854-coming-together-is-the-beginning-keeping-together-is-progress-working.

[16] "A Quote by Nelson Mandela," n.d., https://www. goodreads.com/quotes/270163-do-not-judge-me-by-my-successes-judge-me-by.

[17] "A Quote by Winston S. Churchill," n.d., https:// www.goodreads.com/quotes/3270-success-is-not-final-failure-is-not-fatal-it-is.

[18] "A Quote From Little Women," n.d., https://www. goodreads.com/quotes/52167-love-is-a-great-beautifier.

[19] Donna Sarkar, "20 Brilliant Quotes From Albert Einstein, the Theoretical Physicist Who Became World Famous," Discover Magazine, March 14, 2023, https:// www.discovermagazine.com/the-sciences/20-brilliant-quotes-from-albert-einstein-the-theoretical-physicist-who.

[20] Mar and Mar, "Famous Quotes," Once in a Lifetime Journey, July 29, 2021, https://www. onceinalifetimejourney.com/inspiration/famous-quotes/.

[21] "A Quote From a Letter Addressed to the Abbe Raynal on the Affairs of North America," n.d., https:// www.goodreads.com/quotes/101600-the-mind-once-

enlightened-cannot-again-become-dark.

[22] Fiona Tapp and Ariel Zeitlin, "22 Most Beautiful Proverbs From Around the World," Reader's Digest, August 15, 2021, accessed February 10, 2024, https://www.rd.com/list/proverbs-about-life/.

[23] "A Quote by Steve Jobs," n.d., https://www.goodreads.com/quotes/903982-you-ve-got-to-find-what-you-love-and-that-is.

[24] "A Quote by Albert Einstein," n.d., https://www.goodreads.com/quotes/32930-look-deep-into-nature-and-then-you-will-understand-everything.

[25] "No Man Is an Island – a Selection From the Prose Quotes by John Donne," n.d., https://www.goodreads.com/work/quotes/6791114-no-man-is-an-island.

[26] Wikipedia contributors, "Man Proposes, God Disposes," Wikipedia, November 13, 2023, https://en.wikipedia.org/wiki/Man_Proposes,_God_Disposes.

[27] "A Quote by Aristotle," n.d., https://www.goodreads.com/quotes/103862-it-is-during-our-darkest-moments-that-we-must-focus.

[28] "Where Did the Saying "People Who Live...," Almanac. com, n.d., https://www.almanac.com/fact/where-did-the-saying-people-who-live.

[29] "A Quote by Swedish Proverb," n.d., https://www. goodreads.com/quotes/869108-those-who-wish-to-sing-always-find-a-song.

[30] Fiona Tapp and Ariel Zeitlin, "22 Most Beautiful Proverbs From Around the World," Reader's Digest, August 15, 2021, accessed February 10, 2024, https://www. rd.com/list/proverbs-about-life/.

[31] "NOVA | Einstein's Big Idea | Einstein Quotes (non-Flash) | PBS," n.d., https://www.pbs.org/wgbh/nova/einstein/wisd-nf.html.

[32] By Alison Gee, "Who First Said 'The Pen Is Mightier Than the Sword'?," BBC News, January 9, 2015, https:// www.bbc.com/news/magazine-30729480.

[33] "edwardCoke - Roger Williams National Memorial (U.S. National Park Service)," n.d., https://www.nps.gov/rowi/learn/historyculture/edwardcoke.htm.

[34] Wikipedia contributors, "The Moon Is Made of Green Cheese," Wikipedia, January 24, 2024, https://en.wikipedia.org/wiki/The_Moon_is_made_of_green_cheese.

[35] "William Shakespeare, the Tempest, ACT III, SCENE II," n.d., http://www.perseus.tufts.edu/hopper/t?doc=Perseus%3Atext%3A1999.03.0056%3Aact%3D3%3Ascene%3D2.

[36] "A Quote by Benjamin Franklin," n.d., https://www.goodreads.com/quotes/33937-early-to-bed-and-early-to-rise-makes-a-man.

[37] "As You Like It - Act 3, Scene 2 | Folger Shakespeare Library," Folger, n.d., https://www.folger.edu/explore/shakespeares-works/as-you-like-it/read/3/2/.

[38] "The Ballad of East and West," The Kipling Society, May 14, 2023, https://www.kiplingsociety.co.uk/poem/poems_eastwest.htm.

[39] "A Quote by Albert Einstein," n.d., https://www.goodreads.com/quotes/443233-a-happy-man-is-too-satisfied-with-the-present-to.

[40] Fiona Tapp and Ariel Zeitlin, "22 Most Beautiful Proverbs From Around the World," Reader's Digest, August 15, 2021, accessed February 10, 2024, https://www.rd.com/list/proverbs-about-life/.

[41] "Eat, Drink and Be Merry for Tomorrow We Die - Wiktionary, the Free Dictionary," Wiktionary, n.d., https://en.wiktionary.org/wiki/eat,_drink_and_be_merry_for_tomorrow_we_die.

[42] "A Quote by Benjamin Franklin," n.d., https://www.goodreads.com/quotes/626466-for-the-want-of-a-nail-the-shoe-was-lost.

[43] "A Quote by Albert Einstein," n.d., https://www.goodreads.com/quotes/29213-life-is-like-riding-a-bicycle-to-keep-your-balance.

[44] Wikipedia contributors, "List of Proverbial Phrases," Wikipedia, February 10, 2024, https://en.wikipedia.org/wiki/List_of_proverbial_phrases#G.

[45] "A Quote From Man and Superman," n.d., https://www.goodreads.com/quotes/41390-he-who-can-does-he-who-cannot-teaches.

[46] BookBrowse, "Why Do We Say He Who Laughs Last Laughs Best?," BookBrowse.com, n.d., https://www.bookbrowse.com/expressions/detail/index.cfm/expression_number/360/he-who-laughs-last-laughs-best.

[47] Wikipedia contributors, "Live by the Sword, Die by the Sword," Wikipedia, February 9, 2024, https://en.wikipedia.org/wiki/Live_by_the_sword,_die_by_the_sword.

[48] "Hindsight Is 20/20 - Wiktionary, the Free Dictionary," Wiktionary, n.d., https://en.wiktionary.org/wiki/hindsight_is_20/20.

[49] Fiona Tapp and Ariel Zeitlin, "22 Most Beautiful Proverbs From Around the World," Reader's Digest, August 15, 2021, accessed February 10, 2024, https://www.rd.com/list/proverbs-about-life/.

[50] M Zakirul Karim, "'Peanuts' and 'Monkeys' Effect in Healthcare! Reforming Culture, Controlling Voice?," July 31, 2018, https://www.linkedin.com/pulse/peanuts-monkeys-effect-healthcare-reforming-culture-voice-karim.

[51] Npr, "A Blissful, Timeless Exploration of Human 'Ignorance,'" NPR, August 22, 2009, https://www.npr.org/transcripts/112108819.

[52] "A Quote From Ballads and Other Poems," n.d., https://www.goodreads.com/quotes/21185-be-still-sad-heart-and-cease-repining-behind-the-clouds.

[53] "A Quote From Julius Caesar," n.d., https://www.goodreads.com/quotes/641059-but-for-my-own-part-it-was-greek-to-me.

[54] Augusta Admin, "'It Is Better to Light a Candle Than Curse the Darkness' – Eleanor Roosevelt | Augusta Memorial Public Library," February 26, 2021, https://augustalibrary.org/2021/02/26/it-is-better-to-light-a-candle-than-curse-the-darkness-eleanor-roosevelt/.

[55] "Twelfth Night - Act 3, Scene 4 | Folger Shakespeare Library," Folger, n.d., https://www.folger.edu/explore/shakespeares-works/twelfth-night/read/3/4/.

[56] "SCENE I. the Forest.," n.d., http://shakespeare.mit.edu/asyoulikeit/asyoulikeit.4.1.html.

[57] Ryan Holiday, "Whatever It Is, It's Not a Big Deal," Daily

Stoic, August 2, 2017, https://dailystoic.com/whatever-it-is-it-is-not-a-big-deal/.

[58] "A Quote From David Copperfield," n.d., https://www.goodreads.com/quotes/437231-least-said-soonest-mended.

[59] "A Quote by C.G. Jung," n.d., https://www.goodreads.com/quotes/4483092-life-really-does-begin-at-forty-up-until-then-you.

[60] "As You Like It - Entire Play | Folger Shakespeare Library," Folger, n.d., https://www.folger.edu/explore/shakespeares-works/as-you-like-it/read/.

[61] "A Quote From Tom Brown's Schooldays," n.d., https://www.goodreads.com/quotes/8014816-life-isn-t-all-beer-and-skittles-but-beer-and-skittles.

[62] "A Quote by Eleanor Roosevelt," n.d., https://www.goodreads.com/quotes/51857-life-is-what-you-make-it-always-has-been-always.

[63] "A Quote From Henry VIII," n.d., https://www.goodreads.com/quotes/40729-men-s-evil-manners-live-in-brass-their-virtues-we-write.

[64] Wolfgang Mieder, "'Little Pitchers Have Big Ears': The Intricate World of Children and Proverbs," January 1, 2017, https://scholarworks.iu.edu/journals/index.php/cfr/article/view/25075.

[65] "William Horman Quotes (Author of Vulgaria)," n.d., https://www.goodreads.com/author/quotes/989588. William_Horman.

[66] "Where Does the Expression 'Money Talks' Come From?," English Language & Usage Stack Exchange, n.d., https://english.stackexchange.com/questions/517689/where-does-the-expression-money-talks-come-from.

[67] "A Quote by Milton Berle," n.d., https://www.goodreads.com/quotes/127307-if-opportunity-doesn-t-knock-build-a-door.

[68] "A Quote From as You Like It," n.d., https://www.goodreads.com/quotes/152213-no-sooner-met-but-they-looked-no-sooner-looked-but.

[69] "Only Fools and Horses Work - Wiktionary, the Free Dictionary," Wiktionary, n.d., https://en.wiktionary.org/wiki/only_fools_and_horses_work.

[70] Wikipedia contributors, "List of Proverbial Phrases," Wikipedia, February 10, 2024, https://en.wikipedia.org/wiki/List_of_proverbial_phrases.

[71] "A Quote From as You Like It," n.d., https://www.goodreads.com/quotes/71-the-fool-doth-think-he-is-wise-but-the-wise.

[72] Ajeyaseelan, "147 John Heywood 1497?-1580? John Bartlett - Collection at Bartleby.com," Collection at Bartleby.com, February 27, 2023, https://www.bartleby.com/lit-hub/familiar-quotations/147-john-heywood-1497-1580-john-bartlett/.

[73] "A Quote by William Shakespeare," n.d., https://www.goodreads.com/quotes/21269-they-say-best-men-are-molded-out-of-faults-and.

[74] "A Quote by Confucius," n.d., https://www.goodreads.com/quotes/661227-tell-me-and-i-will-forget-show-me-and-i.

[75] "A Quote by Elbert Hubbard," n.d., https://www.goodreads.com/quotes/740383-when-life-gives-you-lemons-make-lemonade.

www.ingramcontent.com/pod-product-compliance
Lightning Source LLC
Chambersburg PA
CBHW071012120626
46546CB00003B/1044